Short Stories by Jesus
Leader Guide

Short Stories by Jesus:
The Enigmatic Parables of a Controversial Rabbi

Short Stories by Jesus: Participant Guide

978-1-5018-5816-1
978-1-5018-5817-8 eBook

Short Stories by Jesus: Leader Guide

978-1-5018-5818-5
978-1-5018-5819-2 eBook

Short Stories by Jesus: DVD

978-1-5018-5820-8

Short Stories by Jesus:
The Enigmatic Parables of a Controversial Rabbi

978-0-06-156103-0 Paperback
978-0-06-219819-8 eBook

Amy-Jill Levine

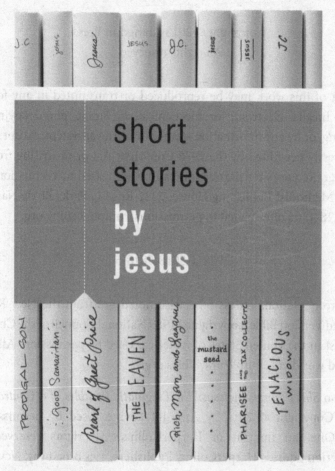

short
stories
by
jesus

The Enigmatic Parables of a Controversial Rabbi

Leader Guide
by Michael S. Poteet

Abingdon Press / Nashville

SHORT STORIES BY JESUS
The Enigmatic Parables of a Controversial Rabbi
Leader Guide

Copyright © 2018 Abingdon Press
All rights reserved.

No part of this work may be reproduced or transmitted in any form or by any means, electronic or mechanical, including photocopying and recording, or by any information storage or retrieval system, except as may be expressly permitted by the 1976 Copyright Act or in writing from the publisher. Requests for permission can be addressed to Permissions, The United Methodist Publishing House, 2222 Rosa L. Parks Blvd., Nashville, TN 37228-1306 or e-mailed to permissions@umpublishing.org.

978-1-5018-5818-5

Scripture quotations unless otherwise noted are from the New Revised Standard Version Bible, copyright © 1989 National Council of the Churches of Christ in the United States of America. Used by permission. All rights reserved worldwide. http://nrsvbibles.org/

Based on *Short Stories by Jesus: The Enigmatic Parables of a Controversial Rabbi.* Copyright © 2014 by Amy-Jill Levine. Used by permission of HarperOne, an imprint of HarperCollins. All rights reserved. For information address HarperCollins Publishers, 195 Broadway, New York, NY 10007. http://www.harpercollins.com

18 19 20 21 22 23 24 25 26 27 — 10 9 8 7 6 5 4 3 2 1
MANUFACTURED IN THE UNITED STATES OF AMERICA

Contents

Introduction

In *Short Stories by Jesus: The Enigmatic Parables of a Controversial Rabbi*, New Testament scholar Amy-Jill Levine invites readers to reconsider several familiar parables—recorded in the Gospels of Matthew, Mark, and Luke—in hopes they will discover how challenging these stories actually are.

"What makes the parables mysterious, or difficult," she writes, "is that they challenge us to look into the hidden aspects of our own values, our own lives. They bring to the surface unasked questions, and they reveal the answers we have always known, but refuse to acknowledge.... Therefore, if we hear a parable and think, 'I really like that,' or, worse, fail to take any challenge, we are not listening well enough."

For each of the parables she discusses, Levine:

- provides a new, "fairly literal" translation in order to make us read the text as though for the first time;
- situates the parable in its original, first-century Jewish context so we can appreciate what Jesus's original audience would and would not have heard in it;
- distinguishes the parables themselves, in as close as we can get to their original forms, from the Gospel writers' initial (and now canonical) interpretations of them;

- exposes the anti-Jewish interpretations—sometimes unintentional and subtle, at other times blatant and ill-intentioned—that have grown up around the parables through centuries of Christian interpretation;
- opens engaging and provocative avenues to fresh interpretations, relevant to modern living.

This Leader Guide is for adults leading groups who are studying *Short Stories by Jesus*. Leaders will find it most helpful to have read Dr. Levine's book, or at least the chapters covered in this study. Leaders will also want to be familiar with the accompanying Participant Guide.

Each session in this Leader Guide includes:

- stated objectives;
- a personal prayer of preparation and tips for leader preparation;
- an opening activity or discussion related to the themes of the session;
- a series of questions designed to engage participants with the parable, related Scripture, and Levine's book;
- opening and closing prayers.

Over the course of this study, you will invite learners to new appreciations of the following parables:

Session 1—"Lost Sheep, Lost Coin, Lost Son"

In the first session, after introducing your group's members to the nature of parables as well as to Dr. Levine's approach to studying Jesus's parables, you will help them examine the three parables in Luke 15 that involve something or someone being lost: the Lost Sheep (Luke 15:4-7), the Lost Coin (Luke 15:8-10), and the Lost Son (Luke 15:11-32). You will help them consider what "taking count" of who and what may be "lost" or missing from a community looks like in your own setting.

Session 2—"The Good Samaritan"

In this session, you will help participants engage with the historical and cultural settings that would have influenced how Jesus's original audience heard this story, recorded for us in Luke 10:25-37. You will examine not only the story itself but also the narrative frame in which Luke has placed it, and you will consider how the frame interprets the story. You will also challenge participants to think concretely about what loving an enemy looks like in today's world.

Session 3—"The Pearl of Great Price"

In this session, your group turns its attention from longer parables to one of Jesus's shortest, preserved in Matthew 13:45-46. You will consider how this parable provokes hearers, in Jesus's day and today, to identify and prioritize valuable "treasure" in their own lives. You will gain further insight into the parable as you compare and contrast it with Matthew's account of Jesus's encounter with a rich, would-be follower (19:16-30). And you will lead your group in putting into words some of the "alternative standards" that identify the kingdom of heaven.

Session 4—"The Mustard Seed"

In this session, you and your group members will practice comparing and contrasting variant versions of the same parable (found in Mark 4:30-32, Matthew 13:31-32, and Luke 13:18-19). You will also study similar images that Jesus used to describe God's kingdom (leaven in Matthew 13:33 and Luke 13:20-21 and a growing seed in Mark 4:26-29), and you will gain an appreciation of how a range of images can enhance our understanding of Jesus's teaching. You will also consider how to discern when faithfulness to God and God's kingdom involves taking direct action and when it involves patient trust in God's action.

Session 5—"The Laborers in the Vineyard"

In this session, you and your group will study Jesus's parable (Matthew 20:1-16) on two levels. You will consider its spiritual lessons by exploring Scriptural associations of a vineyard with God's people, and you will weigh its concrete, practical economic applications. You and participants will think about what economically generous actions you will take in your own lives to express your faithfulness to God.

Session 6—"The Widow and the Judge"

In the final session, you and your group will study one of Jesus's most enigmatic and morally ambiguous parables (Luke 18:1-8). You will consider the parable both within and outside of Luke's narrative frame for it. You will spend time examining biblical images of and stories about widows, and will explore what we gain when we reject stereotypes (even those that may be inspired by Scripture) in favor of viewing and engaging with other people as individuals. You will also have the chance to explore both the problem of judging others and the difference between justice and vengeance.

May you find this Leader Guide informative and helpful as you lead your group toward a richer appreciation of the parables and a closer relationship with the one who told them.

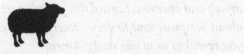

Session 1

Lost Sheep, Lost Coin, Lost Son

SESSION GOALS

This session's reading, discussion, reflection, and prayer will equip participants to:

- deepen relationships with fellow participants;
- reevaluate ideas about the nature and purpose of parables;
- consider potential obstacles in interpreting Jesus's parables;
- practice reading and interpreting Jesus's parables as stories *before*—but not *instead of*—interpreting them as Scripture;
- explore the three parables in **Luke 15**;
- practice "counting" who is missing from their personal relationships and their communities of faith;
- plan and commit to at least one way of seeking whom and what they count as "lost."

SUGGESTED LEADER PREPARATION

Jesus my teacher, grant me curiosity and faithful imagination, patience with myself and openness toward this group's participants, a passion to learn more about Scripture and to grow closer to you, and strength to act on the truths you reveal to us in our study. Amen.

- Carefully and prayerfully read **Luke 15** in one sitting, several times, before the session. Note words and phrases that attract your attention and meditate on them. Write down questions about your reading and try to find answers. If desired, consult a trusted Bible commentary.
- Carefully read *Short Stories by Jesus*, Introduction and chapter 1. Note any material about which you need or want to do further research before the session.
- Carefully read Session 1 of the Participant Guide. Write down any questions or observations the material prompts.
- Secure and prepare a comfortable meeting space for your group, easily accessible to all participants regardless of physical ability.
- Materials needed: Bibles (especially in reputable translations not usually used by your group); one or more standard English dictionaries; recent issues of a local newspaper; recent printed church bulletins and newsletters (if available). *Optional:* name tags, hymnals, light refreshments.
- Have a markerboard or pad of large paper on hand for writing down participants' responses, questions, and insights.
- Choose which discussion questions and activities you will use, keeping in mind your group's interests, previous Bible study experience, and comfort level with academic study (as opposed to purely devotional reading) of Scripture.
- *Optional:* Display three groups of pennies (or other small objects—small candies, for example) side by side on a table where all will be able to see: one group of 100, a second of 10, and a pair.

AS YOUR GROUP GATHERS

Welcome the participants. Ask each to fill out and wear a name tag (*optional*). Ask participants to introduce themselves and to talk briefly about why they are interested in this study of Amy-Jill Levine's *Short Stories by Jesus*. Be ready to talk about why you are interested in facilitating the group, as well!

Optional: Invite participants to look at the three piles of pennies you prepared. Ask them to close their eyes for a moment. Remove one penny from each pile. Ask participants to open their eyes and tell you how the piles are now different.

Tell participants that in today's session they will read and reflect on three of Jesus's parables that involve counting and noticing what, and who, is missing.

Open with this prayer or pray in your own words:

God of all wisdom, you are at work in our world and in our hearts to bring forth a new world and to give us new hearts, in which your will is done on earth as it is in heaven. By your Spirit, teach us in this time together, that we may learn and do all that is needed to receive your rule of grace, for we ask in the name of our Teacher and Savior, Jesus Christ. Amen.

DISCUSS THE NATURE AND PURPOSE OF PARABLES

Ask participants: "What is a parable?" Write responses on a large sheet of paper or markerboard.

Invite one or more participants to look up and read aloud the definitions of *parable* in a standard English dictionary (or from a trusted dictionary website). Ask: "What about these definitions of *parable* seems familiar or unfamiliar to you, and why?"

Read aloud the following list of information, inviting participants to respond to each with any questions or concerns. Make note of any such responses so they are not lost as you continue the study.

- Parables compare two unlike things by putting them side by side in an unexpected way.
- Parables can vary in length from a few sentences to a longer story.
- Parables carry at least two levels of meaning: the literal and the metaphorical.
- Parables may be but are not always allegorical—that is, the elements in a parable do not necessarily represent one and only one other thing or truth.
- Parables do not have a single meaning.
- Jesus did not invent the parable.
- Parables can be interpreted in many ways, but modern readers should always assume a parable's original audience would have been able to find meaning in it; therefore, modern readers must consider the historical and social setting in which a parable originated (in the case of Jesus's parables, first-century Galilee and Judea).

Read aloud this quotation from *Short Stories by Jesus*:

> Jesus was requiring that [his disciples] do more than listen; he was asking them to think as well....What makes the parables mysterious, or difficult, is that they challenge us to look into the hidden aspects of our own values, our own lives. They bring to the surface unasked questions, and they reveal the answers we have always known, but refuse to acknowledge. Our reaction to them should be one of resistance rather than acceptance....
>
> If we hear a parable and think, "I really like that" or, worse, fail to take any challenge, we are not listening well enough....
>
> When we seek universal morals from a genre that is designed to surprise, challenge, shake up, or indict and look for a single meaning in a form that opens to multiple interpretations, we are necessarily limiting the parables and, so, ourselves.

Ask:

- How do you react to Levine's claim that parables should provoke our resistance rather than our acceptance?
- Why might a teacher like Jesus choose to teach using parables?
- Why, according to **Mark 4:10-13**, did Jesus teach in parables? How do you react to this reason?

When [Jesus] was alone, those who were around him along with the twelve asked him about the parables. And he said to them, "To you has been given the secret of the kingdom of God, but for those outside, everything comes in parables; in order that

> *'they may indeed look, but not perceive,*
> *and may indeed listen, but not understand;*
> *so that they may not turn again and be forgiven.'"*

And he said to them, "Do you not understand this parable? Then how will you understand all the parables?"

Mark 4:10-13

IDENTIFY POTENTIAL OBSTACLES
TO INTERPRETING JESUS'S PARABLES

Invite one or two participants to tell a brief story or anecdote about something that happened to someone else and about which they have no firsthand knowledge. Point out that, in a similar way, we have no direct access to Jesus's parables. We only have Matthew's, Mark's, and Luke's presentations of the parables (John's Gospel includes no stories Jesus told). Jesus left no written documents.

Ask about this and other potential obstacles in interpreting Jesus's parables:

- When trying to understand Jesus's parables, why do we need to remember that, as Levine says, "the evangelists are our first known interpreters of the parables"?
- How can the differences between first-century life and culture in Jesus's Galilee and Judea and our twenty-first-century life and culture sometimes make it harder to understand Jesus's parables?
- What can people who've heard and read Jesus's parables many times, perhaps even over a lifetime, do to remain open to new insights into and understandings of these stories?

Compare and Contrast Two Parables

Have participants turn in their Bibles to **Luke 15**. Form two groups of participants. Ask one group to read **verses 3-6 only**. Ask the other to read **verses 8-9 only**. Encourage participants to try and read these verses, as much as possible, as though for the first time, and to consider—for the moment—only their assigned verses. You may wish to have on hand Bibles of a reputable translation your group does not usually use, or you may ask them to use Levine's "fairly literal" translations in *Short Stories by Jesus*—"if the literalness makes the parable seem unfamiliar," Levine writes, "good." Her literal translations can help in listening anew to the parables, and thinking about each of the words Jesus chose to use.

Ask each group to discuss these questions (which you have written on a large sheet of paper or markerboard) about their assigned readings:

- Who is the protagonist (the character in a story who struggles to overcome a problem)?
- What is the problem?
- How and how far is the protagonist's problem resolved?
- What specific words, images, and details of plot and character do you notice?
- What questions do you have about this story?

Note: Treating biblical texts, let alone stories told by Jesus, as the fictional stories they are before interpreting those stories as Scripture may feel uncomfortable, even upsetting, to some participants. You can suggest to them that while Christians believe Jesus was (and is) much more than a devout, intelligent, and creative first-century rabbi, he was not *less*, and he expected his hearers to engage with the parables *as* stories. Suggest that, in the interaction between hearer and story, the Word of God begins to be heard.

After allowing sufficient time for discussion, invite each group to report its findings to the whole group. Encourage participants to point out similarities and differences between the two parables.

Ask:

- What is lost in each story, and why?
- What do the protagonists' reactions to these losses, and to the findings, suggest about them?
- Forgetting for the moment the interpretations offered in Luke 15, what would you say these stories were "about"? Why?

Read aloud **Luke 15:7** and **15:10**. Ask:

- Levine writes that Luke interprets these two parables from Jesus as being about repentance and forgiveness. She also notes that sheep and coins do not repent, and the sheep owner and the woman who find their lost objects do not forgive them. To the contrary, the problem is that they lost the objects. Based on your studies of the stories themselves, how much sense does this interpretation about repenting and forgiving make to you? Why or why not?

OPTIONAL CREATIVE EXTENSION: REWRITE THE PARABLES

Invite participants to write a diary entry or letter from either the sheep owner or the woman's point of view. How would these characters talk about what happened in their own words? Invite volunteers to share their responses.

Ask:

- How does this creative exercise help readers "enter into" the world of Jesus's stories? What obstacles to entering that world remain?
- How do such creative retellings reveal as much (if not more) about the storyteller as the stories themselves?
- Do creative responses like these help or hinder our understanding of the parables as Scripture, and why?

READ AND DISCUSS THE PARABLE OF THE LOST SON

Recruit four volunteers to read aloud **Luke 15:11-32**. They will read as the narrator (Jesus), the younger son, the father, and the older son.

After the reading, ask:

- On a scale of 1-5 (where "1" = "never even heard of it" and "5" = "I could recite it in my sleep"), how familiar were you with this parable before the reading?
- What interpretations, lessons and morals, or applications have you drawn from this parable in the past, or have you heard preachers and Bible teachers draw? What do you think of these interpretations?
- With which character in this parable do you most identify, and why? With which character do you least identify, and why?
- Levine points out that Jewish sources do not support the commonly repeated idea that the younger son sinned in asking for his share of the inheritance, or that he "treated his father as if he were as good as dead." What do you think about the son's request? What do you think about the father's choice to "divide his life" (Levine's literal translation of verse 12) between them?

- Levine also points out that the parable does not support the idea that the younger son sinned in working with pigs in Gentile territory. He did not eat the pigs (Leviticus 11:7-8). "The prodigal is in an impossible situation," she writes, "but the issue is not Jewish xenophobia or purity. The problem is starvation." When have you found yourself in an "impossible situation," doing whatever you must to get through?

- Is the younger son truly sorry for having left home and wasted his half of the inheritance, or is he planning a practical way out of his predicament (verses 17-19)? Why do you think as you do?

- Levine writes, "Jewish fathers of the first century were not, at least according to the sources we have (which should be the sources that inform our history), distant or wrathful." What do you make of the father's reaction to the younger son's return (verses 20-24; compare 15:6, 9)?

- How much sympathy do you have for the elder son's reaction to the younger son's return (verses 25-30)? Why?

- Levine suggests the father in this parable is like the sheep owner and the woman in the previous two parables because he lost something—or, more accurately, *someone*. How did the father "lose" his oldest son? What do you think of his efforts to "find" the oldest son again (verses 31-32)?

- We can infer from Luke's placement of this parable immediately after the parables of the Lost Sheep and Lost Coin that Luke wanted to read it, too, as mostly a story about repentance and heavenly joy. What other meanings do you see in the parable when you examine it independently? To what extent do these multiple meanings contradict or complement each other?

CALL TO ACTION

Read aloud this quotation from *Short Stories by Jesus*:

> We need to take count not only of our blessings, but also of those in our families, and in our communities. And once we count, we need to act. Finding the lost, whether they are sheep, coins, or people, takes work. It also requires our efforts, and from those efforts there is the potential for wholeness and joy.

Distribute recent issues of a local newspaper to participants. Invite them to spend a few minutes looking through its pages for groups and people who receive little or no attention. Who is missing? (For example: How many stories are about people who are homeless? people who are poor or sick? children? people of ethnic minorities in your area?)

Brainstorm a list of these groups and people on a large sheet of paper or markerboard.

Then ask participants to look at recent bulletins (orders of service) and/or newsletters, as available, from your congregation with the same question in mind: Who is missing? Based on this document, to whom does it appear we minister? (For example: Are members who are homebound listed? members who are not in the majority age or ethnic group? nonmembers from the community who have some other connection to your church? children?) Brainstorm a list of these groups and people on a large sheet of paper or markerboard.

Tip: If these printed resources aren't available, browse the local newspaper's and your congregation's websites. Who is pictured and discussed? Who is not?

Ask:

- What more could our congregation be doing to connect with and serve those both within and without our own community of faith who appear "missing" or "lost"?

- How can we make the ways in which we do reach out to the "missing" and "lost" more visible within and without our own congregation?

CLOSING PRAYER

You know us all, Lord Jesus, and you know those whom we do not. Forgive us when we lose those who are precious to you, by what we do or by what we fail to do. Send us in your Spirit's power to them, that we may rejoice together as children of your Father in heaven, and ours. Amen.

Session 2

The Good Samaritan

SESSION GOALS

This session's reading, discussion, reflection, and prayer will equip participants to:

- identify ways in which church and culture use the phrase "good Samaritan";
- explore the parable in **Luke 10:25-37** and the context in which Luke recorded it;
- appreciate the historic relationship between Jews and Samaritans;
- imagine modern analogues of Jesus's parable;
- evaluate their own willingness to get involved in helping people who need their help.

SUGGESTED LEADER PREPARATION

Jesus my teacher, as you challenged your followers' preconceptions about whom they should see as their neighbors, so challenge this group and challenge me as together we strive to hear and obey your call to love others. Amen.

- Carefully and prayerfully read **Luke 10:25-37** in one sitting, several times, before the session. Note words and phrases that attract your attention and meditate on them. Write down questions about your reading and try to find answers. If desired, consult a trusted Bible commentary.
- Carefully read *Short Stories by Jesus*, chapter 2. Note any material about which you need or want to do further research before the session.
- Carefully read Session 2 of the Participant Guide. Write down any questions or observations the material prompts.
- Secure and prepare a comfortable meeting space for your group, easily accessible to all participants regardless of physical ability.
- Materials needed: Bibles (especially in reputable translations not usually used by your group), biblical reference works such as one or more Bible atlas and Bible dictionary. *Optional:* name tags, hymnals, light refreshments.
- Have a markerboard or pad of large paper on hand for writing down participants' responses, questions, and insights.
- Choose which discussion questions and activities you will use, keeping in mind your group's interests, previous Bible study experience, and comfort level with academic study (as opposed to purely devotional reading) of Scripture.

AS YOUR GROUP GATHERS

Welcome participants. Ask each to fill out and wear a name tag *(optional)*. Especially welcome any new participants. Review the first session by asking those who attended:

- What is a parable? *(a short story or saying that teaches by means of comparison and challenges its audience's preconceptions)*
- Who were the first interpreters of Jesus's parables? *(Matthew, Mark, and Luke)*

23

- What is one new insight you gained from our study in the session of Jesus's parables of the Lost Sheep, the Lost Coin, and the Lost Son?

Invite all participants to define the phrase "good Samaritan." *Optional:* Ask participants with smartphones to use a search engine feature such as Google News to find current examples of the phrase. Ask how these examples reinforce, refine, or challenge participants' definition of the phrase.

Tell participants (as they have probably guessed) they will be studying the parable usually titled "The Good Samaritan" in today's session. Now that they have identified their own and their culture's common understanding of that phrase, encourage them to set it aside as much as possible during the session in order to encourage a fresh encounter with the story Jesus told and the messages God is communicating through it.

Open with this prayer or pray in your own words:

Merciful God, compassionate and gracious: you call us to show mercy to others even as you have shown mercy to us in Jesus Christ. Now, by your Spirit, open our minds to new insights into what being merciful means, and open our hearts and our eyes to all those to whom you would have us give mercy—and from whom you would have us receive it. This we ask for the sake of Jesus our Savior. Amen.

STUDY THE SAMARITANS

Allow participants time to research Samaria and Samaritans in biblical reference works like a Bible atlas or Bible dictionary, or on a trusted biblical studies website. Encourage any participants using study Bibles to consult the maps or other study helps those Bibles contain. After allowing sufficient time for research, invite volunteers to talk briefly about something they discovered about Samaria or the Samaritans that interests them.

Supplement participants' findings with information from the following list of bullet points about Samaria and the Samaritans. Invite participants to comment on any information that strikes them as particularly noteworthy.

- In the ninth and eighth centuries BCE, Samaria was the capital of the Northern Kingdom (Israel). Jerusalem, the "city of David," was the capital of the Southern Kingdom, Judah.
- King Ahab built a temple to Baal in Samaria (1 Kings 16:29-33)...which King Jehu later destroyed and turned into "a latrine" (2 Kings 10:27).
- During the reign of Israel's King Ahaz, Israel attacked Judah and took 200,000 Judeans captive. The prophet Oded in Samaria told the Israelites to send the Judeans back home, which they did (2 Chronicles 28:8-15).
- The Assyrians conquered Samaria in 722 BCE, and the Northern Kingdom's people were exiled or assimilated into non-Israelite peoples (2 Kings 17:21-24), becoming the so-called "Ten Lost Tribes of Israel"; the Northern Kingdom, now known as "Samaria," was populated by members of the ten tribes who remained coupled with others whom the Assyrians relocated into the area.
- When former exiles in Babylon returned to Jerusalem (circa 538 BCE) and started rebuilding the Temple, they experienced hostility from people living in the region of Samaria (Nehemiah 4:1-8).
- Jews who rebelled around 165 BCE against Antiochus IV Epiphanes resented the Samaritans for not helping them.
- In Jesus's day, suspicion and resentment between Jews and Samaritans persisted (Matthew 10:5; Luke 9:51-55; John 4:9).
- Samaritans call themselves *Shomrim* or *Shamerim*—"guardians" or "observers" of the Law—and believe the Northern Kingdom sanctuary at Mt. Gerizim taught the correct interpretation of Torah.
- Samaritans accept only their version of the Pentateuch (the Bible's first five books) as authoritative; their Scripture does not include the Prophets or the Writings.

Read aloud this quotation from *Short Stories by Jesus*:

> The problem with [the label "good Samaritan"] is not simply
> a lack of sensitivity toward the Samaritan people—yes, there
> are still Samaritans. It is also a lack of awareness of how odd
> the expression "good Samaritan" would have seemed to Jesus's
> Jewish contemporaries.

READ THE PARABLE

Have participants turn in their Bibles to Luke 10. Recruit a volunteer to
read aloud **only verses 30-35** while others follow along. (As in the previous
session, you may wish to have on hand Bibles of a reputable translation
your group does not usually use, or you may ask them to use Amy-Jill
Levine's "fairly literal" translation in *Short Stories by Jesus*.)

Ask:

- How much or how little do we know *from the parable itself* about
  each of the following characters:
  ◊ the man who was attacked?
  ◊ the people who attacked him?
  ◊ the priest?
  ◊ the Levite?
  ◊ the Samaritan?
- What might we wish to know about any or all of these characters
  that we can only guess at or imagine because of a lack of evidence
  in the story?
- When, if ever, have you heard some of these guesses or
  imaginings taught as important for understanding this story?
- Some imaginative "filling in the blanks" is necessary for
  understanding many fictional stories, including Jesus's parables.
  How do we determine whether our imaginations are helping or
  hindering us in understanding a parable?

- Why does the parable specifically state that the priest, Levite, and Samaritan all saw the man who had been attacked (verses 31-33)?
- Levine surveys Jewish scripture, tradition, and historical sources to conclude that first-century Jewish Law required both the priest and Levite to stop and try to help the man: "Their responsibility was to save a life; they failed." Even had they thought the man was dead, they should have stopped to bury him. What does this fact suggest about the Law, and about the priest and Levite?
- In folklore, according to Levine, the "rule of three" "uses two models [in a story] to set up a third, and the third creates the variation on the theme." (Think about Goldilocks and the Three Bears, for example.) How does this parable follow the rule of three? What effect does the pattern have?
- Why does the parable describe the Samaritan's actions in greater detail than the priest's or Levite's actions (verses 33-34)?
- How do these other verses from the Gospels help us define "compassion" (*splagchnizomai*)? (You may wish to tell participants this word derives from the Greek word for "the bowels"—the "guts," we might say—which were believed to be the bodily organ of emotions, as modern people talk colloquially of the heart. Compassion was thus felt "in the gut," as we might say we feel it "in our heart of hearts.")
  ◊ Luke 7:13
  ◊ Luke 15:20
  ◊ Mark 1:41
  ◊ Mark 9:22
  ◊ Matthew 15:32
- Based on what you studied earlier in this session about the historic relationship between Jews and Samaritans, how do you imagine a first-century Jewish audience would react to this parable told by Jesus, a first-century Jewish teacher, and why?

- How do the good Samaritan's actions mirror what Samaritans did to the Judean captives in 2 Chronicles 28:8-15? How does this story from Hebrew Scripture add significance to Jesus's parable?
- What would you say this parable is "about"? Why?

Examine Luke's "Frame" for the Parable

Remind participants that in *Short Stories by Jesus*, Levine encourages readers to consider Jesus's parables themselves, so far as we are able, before interpreting them in light of the contexts in which the evangelists have recorded them. Point out that the evangelists intended these settings to influence their readers to interpret the parables in certain ways.

Note: If needed, assure participants this approach does not suggest malevolence or any intent to deceive on the evangelists' part. It simply recognizes that all artistic texts—and the Gospels are artfully arranged selections and presentations of actual events (see Luke 1:1-4; John 20: 30-31; John 21:24-25)—have a point of view. We might think of the evangelists as pastors or priests who interpret their Scripture in light of the needs and concerns of their congregations. They are thus the first interpreters of the parables. Their interpretations are not wrong, but neither are they the only ones we can find.

Explain that Luke has recorded this parable using a literary technique known as a "framing story." As a frame holds a window in place so people can see through it, a framing story surrounds another story so that readers can see into it. The framing story frequently influences how audiences hear and understand the central story.

Recruit two more volunteers to read aloud **verses 25-29** and **verses 36-37**—one reading the verses containing the lawyer's words, the other reading the verses containing Jesus's words—and have the original volunteer again read the parable aloud (verses 30-35) in between.

Ask:

- Levine notes, "For Jesus's Jewish audience, lawyers would likely have been positive figures and their connection to the Torah a good thing." How does Luke indicate that *this* lawyer is not to be viewed positively?

- Read **Leviticus 18:1-5** and **Deuteronomy 30:15-16**. How do these Scriptures help us understand how and why Jesus corrects the focus of the lawyer's trick question?
- Read **Leviticus 19:17-18, 33-34**. How does the Scripture make the lawyer's second question, as Levine writes, "not relevant" in the "context of love"?
- Leviticus 19 distinguishes between "neighbors" and "strangers" (or "aliens"), but insists we are to love both. In a Jewish context, the neighbor would be a fellow Jew, and the stranger a Gentile. Who are the strangers in your setting? Can you love the stranger as a stranger, or do you want to make the stranger a neighbor (that is, a fellow Christian)?
- What does Jesus's final exchange with the lawyer (verses 36-37) teach about what it means to love God and to love the neighbor?
- How does Luke's framing story reinforce the meaning(s) found in the parable itself?

IMAGINE MODERN ANALOGIES OF JESUS'S PARABLE

Levine suggests that a "parable of the 'Good Hamas Member'" might be difficult to hear but an appropriate modern version of Jesus's parable. Encourage participants to imagine other hypothetical parables that would affect a modern audience in your group's social context in the same way that Jesus's parable is likely to have affected those who first heard it. Who would the "Good Samaritan" be for people in your community, in your congregation, today? Invite any especially creative and ambitious storytellers in your group to try writing a full version of their parable.

CALL TO ACTION

Read aloud these quotations from *Short Stories by Jesus*:

To ask "Who is my neighbor" is a polite way of asking, "Who is *not* my neighbor?" or "Who does not deserve my love?" or "Whose lack of food or shelter can I ignore?" or "Who can I hate?" The answer Jesus gives is, "No one."

Can we finally agree that it is better to acknowledge the humanity and the potential to do good to the enemy, rather than to choose death? Will we be able to care for our enemies, who are also our neighbors?

Ask participants to think silently about someone—a specific individual, or a type of person—whom they consider (or have considered) an enemy. Then read aloud **Luke 10:27**: *"You shall love the Lord your God with all your heart, and with all your soul, and with all your strength, and with all your mind; and [love] _____ as yourself"*—telling participants to fill in the blank with the enemy they have identified. Read the verse two more times, slowly, allowing time for reflection between repetitions. After the third time, invite participants to visualize themselves performing some concrete act of mercy toward their enemy. Invite any volunteers who wish to share their reflections aloud to do so (should you choose this option, you, as leader, should be prepared to start the sharing).

CLOSING PRAYER

Close with this prayer or in your own words:

Lord Jesus, you command us to love our enemies. Teach us that this love is not so much about what we feel as about what we do, and strengthen us, by your Spirit, to see, to touch, to provide for, to heal, and to care in practical ways for those we may be unable even to bring ourselves to name, that we may be children of your Father in heaven and ours, who causes the sun to rise on the evil and the good and who sends rain to shower both those who are righteous and those who are not. Amen.

Session 3

The Pearl of Great Price

SESSION GOALS

This session's reading, discussion, reflection, and prayer will equip participants to:

- reflect on what they consider to be valuable treasure;
- explore the parable in **Matthew 13:45-46**, both on its own and in the narrative context in which Matthew has placed it (13:44-53);
- compare and contrast the parable to Matthew's record of Jesus's encounter with a rich young man (Matthew 19:16-30);
- point to countercultural acts of assigning ultimate value to things, people, and causes;
- identify what they consider their personal "pearls of great price"—their highest priorities, for which they would give up everything else;
- articulate some of the "alternative standards" that define the shape of the kingdom of heaven.

SUGGESTED LEADER PREPARATION

Jesus my teacher, help me honestly evaluate my own priorities—what they are, and what you would have them be—that this group and I may together learn more about what matters to you, and how to cherish it. Amen.

- Carefully and prayerfully read **Matthew 13:45-46** several times before the session. Note words and phrases that attract your attention and meditate on them. Write down questions about your reading and try to find answers. If desired, consult a trusted Bible commentary.
- Carefully read *Short Stories by Jesus*, chapter 4. Note any material about which you need or want to do further research before the session.
- Carefully read Session 3 of the Participant Guide. Write down any questions or observations the material prompts.
- Secure and prepare a comfortable meeting space for your group, easily accessible to all participants regardless of physical ability.
- Materials needed: Bibles (especially in reputable translations not usually used by your group); quick-drying modeling clay and a toothpick or other stylus-like implement for each participant. *Optional:* name tags, hymnals, light refreshments, images of pearls.
- Have a markerboard or pad of large paper on hand for writing down participants' responses, questions, and insights.
- Choose which discussion questions and activities you will use, keeping in mind your group's interests, previous Bible study experience, and comfort level with academic study (as opposed to purely devotional reading) of Scripture.

AS YOUR GROUP GATHERS

Welcome participants. Ask each to fill out and wear a name tag *(optional)*. Especially welcome any new participants. Invite participants who have attended previous sessions to talk briefly about any new insights they have gained or questions they are continuing to ponder.

Open with this prayer or pray in your own words:

Great God, from whom comes every good and perfect gift: grant us, by your Spirit, a time of discovery and discernment, that we may grow as Jesus's students, learning to become people who can distinguish all in this world that is of true worth and eternal significance. Amen.

THINK ABOUT TREASURE AND PEARLS

Ask participants: "What do you think of as treasure?" Accept and acknowledge all responses.

Next, ask participants to tell you everything they know about or associate with pearls. Write down responses on a large sheet of paper or markerboard. *Optional:* Display images of pearls (or invite participants with smartphones to look up such images) to spur participants' responses.

Read aloud the following statements based on information in *Short Stories by Jesus*, asking participants to vote on whether each is true or false:

- Most people in the ancient Roman Empire would never have seen an actual pearl. *(True)*
- According to the ancient Roman historian Pliny, Cleopatra dissolved a pearl in vinegar and drank it to win a bet with Marc Antony. *(True)*
- Because the oyster that produces a pearl is not kosher (that is, appropriate for observant Jews to eat), pearls are not kosher. *(False. Apart from the fact that kosher is a category that almost always applies to food and drink, pearls are not forbidden under Jewish law.)*
- Pearls are not mentioned in the Old Testament (Hebrew Scriptures). (*True. Amy-Jill Levine says the word in Job 28:18 that the NRSV translates "pearls" means "jewels.")*

Tell participants to keep in mind all these impressions of treasure in general and pearls in particular as they read and study the parable in this session.

READ THE PARABLE

Have participants turn in their Bibles to **Matthew 13**. (As in previous sessions, you may wish to have on hand Bibles of a reputable translation your group does not usually use, or you may ask them to use Levine's "fairly literal" translation in *Short Stories by Jesus*.) Recruit a volunteer to read aloud **Matthew 13:45-46 only**. (*Note:* If needed or desired, refer back to the comments in this Leader Guide, Session 2, regarding the possibility and value of thinking separately, as far as possible, about Jesus's parables and the settings in which the evangelists placed them.)

Ask:

- To whom does this parable compare the kingdom of heaven? Do you think of the comparison as being to the man, to the pearl, or to both together?
- What is the difference between identifying the parable's protagonist as "a man, a merchant" (Levine's translation) and simply "a merchant" (NRSV)? What do we gain and lose in equating this man (or anyone, for that matter) with an occupation?
- Surveying several Bible passages (for example: Genesis 37:28; Revelation 18:11, 15-23), Levine argues that, in both the Old and New Testaments, merchants are "regarded with some suspicion" and that "the entire enterprise of high-end trade receives a negative verdict." How does this background information affect your understanding of the parable?
- What does this person do in the parable?
- How do you characterize the man's choice to sell "all that he had" in order to buy the "one pearl of great value"—something that, as

34

Levine notes, is "a beautiful object, but one that cannot nourish, shelter, or clothe"?

- Levine points out that the man "will stay a person, but he may not stay a merchant." Why is this so? How does the man's action at the end of the parable potentially affect his occupation and identity?
- What does your reading of this parable, in and of itself, suggest to you about the nature of the kingdom of heaven?
- Levine lists some commonly heard interpretations of this parable. Which of these are familiar to you? What other interpretations, not in this list, have you heard from teachers and preachers in the past? Given your close reading of the parable itself, which interpretations seem reasonable to you? Which do not? Why?
  ◊ The pearl represents secret spiritual knowledge (of the Bible, of Christian history, of heavenly wisdom, and so on).
  ◊ The man demonstrates the virtue of sacrifice.
  ◊ The pearl represents Jesus, the Bible, the church, or salvation (everlasting life).

CONSIDER MATTHEW'S CONTEXT FOR THE PARABLE

Form two groups of participants. Ask one group to read and discuss **Matthew 13:44**. Ask the other to read and discuss **Matthew 13:47-50**. After allowing sufficient time, invite each group to briefly compare and contrast the parable it read with the parable in 13:45-46.

Ask:

- How, if at all, do the parables on either side of the one in verses 45-46 shape or change the way you understand it?
- Levine states that, for Matthew, the first two parables (verse 44 and verses 45-46) are about being disciples. How is this so?
- How might the second and third parables (verses 45-46 and verses 47-50) work together, for Matthew, to say something about the future aspect of the kingdom of heaven?

- Read **Matthew 13:51-53**. Levine states, "This last line [of Matthew's narrative setting for these three parables] returns readers to the practical and so the economic." How might the scribes trained for the kingdom be like the characters in any of the three parables?

- Levine points out that the word NRSV translates "brings out" in verse 52 literally means "casts out" (*ekballo*)—the same word used for what Jesus does to demons. In what circumstances would those trained for the kingdom of heaven need to "cast out" treasures?

COMPARE THE PARABLE TO MATTHEW 19:16-30

Have participants turn in their Bibles to **Matthew 19:16-30**. Recruit volunteers to read this passage aloud, taking the roles of a narrator, Jesus, the rich young man, and Peter/the disciples.

Ask:

- How and why does Jesus redirect the man's question to him (verses 16-17)? (You may wish to remind participants of Jesus's redirection of the same question in **Luke 10:25-28**, before the parable of the Good Samaritan.)

- Levine questions whether the young man "really does 'love his neighbor as himself'" because of his "many possessions" (verse 22) and his reaction to Jesus's suggestion that the man sell them to help people who are poor (verse 21). To what extent is a person's wealth a measure of how much they are loving their neighbors?

- Why does Jesus say it is hard for those who are rich to enter the kingdom of heaven? What is it about "many possessions" (verse 22) that gets in their way?

- What does Jesus promise to Peter and those who "have left everything" to follow Jesus (verses 27-30)?

- What connections can you make between this incident in Jesus's life and the parable of the man who sold all he had to acquire the pearl of great value? How does this story shape your understanding of that parable?
- Levine notes that many Christian interpreters decide that Jesus's instruction to divest of all worldly treasure applied *only* to the young man in Matthew 19. Do you agree with this interpretation? Why or why not?

CALL TO ACTION

Read aloud this quotation from *Short Stories by Jesus*:

By the standards of the status quo—whether in first-century Galilee or twenty-first-century America—the merchant has acted in a reckless manner. The merchant, however, sets up alternative standards not determined by society, but determined by something else, whether his own desires or a heavenly prompt. He really is "countercultural." He defines his treasure in his own terms. He is able to recognize what for him has true value, and he can do what he needs to do in order to obtain it.

Ask:

- When have you seen people, whether Christian or not, engage in similarly "countercultural" identifications of what things, people, and causes really matter and have ultimate value? How have you seen these people do whatever it takes to get their "pearls of great price"?
- When have you defined your ultimate treasure on your own terms, regardless of what others said or did? What did you do to pursue it? What happened as a result?
- Are all personal definitions of ultimate value and ultimate treasure equally valid? Why or why not?

- Based on your relationship with Jesus, as well as your knowledge of the Bible and the Christian tradition, what "alternative standards" would you point to as the standards by which God defines the shape of the kingdom of heaven?

Encourage participants to spend a few minutes reflecting on what they consider to be of ultimate value. Ask: "What would you, like the man in Jesus's parable, be willing to get rid of all you have in order to get—even at the risk of changing your identity in your own eyes and the eyes of others?" Be prepared to model honesty by talking about your own response to the question. Invite volunteers to talk about their responses.

You might also wish to read aloud from Levine's experience talking with her students at Riverbend Maximum Security Prison about their "pearls of great price" (*Short Stories by Jesus*, pp. 162–163).[1]

OPTIONAL SESSION EXTENSION ACTIVITIES

Give each participant a lump of quick-drying modeling clay and a toothpick (or other stylus-like implement). Have participants roll the clay into balls, thus creating "pearls." Instruct them to use the toothpick to scratch words or symbols into their pearls that will remind them of what they believe God is calling them to get, even at the cost of getting rid of all else.

CLOSING PRAYER

Close with this prayer or in your own words:

Holy God, through Jesus Christ, your inexpressibly precious gift, you challenged us to give up earthly treasures and to store up for ourselves treasures in heaven, where thieves cannot steal and rust cannot destroy. Challenge us again, this day and every day, to seek what you would most have us find, to your glory and for the good of our neighbor; and may your Spirit keep us strong in answering that challenge, day by day. Amen.

---

1 In this Leader Guide, page references to *Short Stories by Jesus* are from the Paperback edition (2015).

Session 4

The Mustard Seed

SESSION GOALS

This session's reading, discussion, reflection, and prayer will equip participants to:

- Reflect on their firsthand experiences of seeds and gardening, and relate these experiences to Jesus's parables;
- Explore the parables about a mustard seed recorded in **Mark 4:30-32, Matthew 13:31-32**, and **Luke 13:18-19**;
- Respond to common interpretations of the Mustard Seed parable(s) and articulate their own interpretations;
- Appreciate the image of the mustard seed by comparing and contrasting it with Jesus's images of yeast (leaven) (Matthew 13:33; Luke 13:20-21) and growing seed (Mark 4:26-29);
- Apply suggested interpretations of the Mustard Seed parable to situations in contemporary society and in their own lives.

SUGGESTED LEADER PREPARATION

Jesus my teacher, may your Spirit lead our group as we seek to grow in our ability to recognize and respond to God's reign through both obedient action and faithful trust. Amen.

- Carefully and prayerfully read each of these three passages several times before the session: **Mark 4:30-32; Matthew 13:31-32; Luke 13:18-19**. Note words and phrases that attract your attention and meditate on them. Write down questions about your reading and try to find answers. If desired, consult a trusted Bible commentary.
- Carefully read *Short Stories by Jesus*, chapter 5. Note any material about which you need or want to do further research before the session.
- Carefully read Session 4 of the Participant Guide. Write down any questions or observations the material prompts.
- Secure and prepare a comfortable meeting space for your group, easily accessible to all participants regardless of physical ability.
- Materials needed: Bibles (especially in reputable translations not usually used by your group), a variety of loose seeds, scrap paper. *Optional:* name tags, hymnals, light refreshments; seeds, soil, and containers for planting; pine cones, peanut butter, birdseed, yarn.
- Have a markerboard or pad of large paper on hand for writing down participants' responses, questions, and insights.
- Choose which discussion questions and activities you will use, keeping in mind your group's interests, previous Bible study experience, and comfort level with academic study (as opposed to purely devotional reading) of Scripture.

AS YOUR GROUP GATHERS

Welcome participants. Ask each to fill out and wear a name tag *(optional)*. Especially welcome any new participants. Invite participants who have attended previous sessions to talk briefly about any new insights they have gained or questions they are continuing to ponder.

Open with this prayer or pray in your own words:

Creator God, who gives life and growth: we want to see your will be done on earth as in heaven, and we would be those who do it, humbly and joyfully. Through what we read and discuss today, show us when and how we can be agents of your kingdom's growth. Amen.

THINK ABOUT SEEDS AND GARDENING

Hand seeds to participants and invite them to pass them around. Ask for them to talk about their observations of these seeds or the associations seeds in general carry for them. Also ask participants who have experience gardening to talk briefly about what gardeners must do and must not do in order to successfully grow plants and vegetables.

Encourage participants to keep these observations and associations in mind as they read the parables in today's session.

READ THE PARABLES

Recruit three volunteers. Have one volunteer turn to **Mark 4:30-32** in her or his Bible. Have the second turn to **Matthew 13:31-32**. Have the third turn to **Luke 13:18-19**. (As in previous sessions, you may wish to have on hand Bibles of a reputable translation your group does not usually use, or you may ask them to use Amy-Jill Levine's "fairly literal" translation in *Short Stories by Jesus*.)

Ask each volunteer to read aloud his or her assigned passage, one after the other. Then ask participants:

- What three elements do these three parables have in common? (mustard seed, branches, birds taking shelter)
- What details differ among the three parables? (Encourage participants to read the texts closely to find the different details. You may wish to refer to *Short Stories by Jesus*, pp. 165–166, to help participants spot the differences. Many Bible readers tend to harmonize or conflate similar but different texts such as these.)
- How do you account for the similarities and differences among these three parables?
- In *Short Stories by Jesus*, Levine points out that the Greek term for "mustard seed" (*kokkos sinapeos*) "appears nowhere we can locate prior to its use in the Gospels." Why do you imagine Jesus might have chosen to speak specifically about this kind of seed? (You may wish to refer participants to *Short Stories by Jesus*, pp. 177–178: "Since mustard can be planted, and since mustard has medicinal and gastronomical benefits...mustard is exactly the type of crop one wants.")
- In Mark and Matthew, Jesus says the mustard seed is the smallest of all seeds. It is not—nor does it grow into a tree, as Jesus says in Luke. Does Jesus's apparent lack of botanical knowledge present a problem in understanding the parables? Why or why not?
- Find in your Bibles and read these verses that refer, as does the Mustard Seed parable, to "the birds of the air": **Genesis 2:20; Psalm 104:12, 16-17; Ezekiel 31:3-14; Matthew 6:26; Matthew 8:20.** Do you think any or all of these passages might add to our understanding of the parable? If so, how? If not, why not? (You may wish to refer participants to the discussion in *Short Stories by Jesus*, pp. 178–180.)
- Raise your hand if you have ever heard one of these common interpretations of the parables, identified by Levine (you may respond more than once):

◊ The large growth from the small seed represents the miraculous growth of God's kingdom and/or the church.

◊ The birds finding shelter represent the nations being gathered into God's people (Israel and/or the church).

◊ The natural growth from the seed represents the natural, inevitable growth of God's kingdom and/or the church.

◊ The large growth from the seed represents eternal life (salvation).

• What is your opinion of one or more of these common interpretations? Do any of them strike you as more or less plausible or persuasive? Why or why not?

• What other interpretations, if any, of these parables are you familiar with?

• What do the mustard seed parables—any one of them, or all three together—suggest to us about God's kingdom?

COMPARE THE MUSTARD SEED IMAGE TO SIMILAR IMAGES

Tell participants both Matthew and Luke placed the mustard seed parable directly before another of Jesus's parables that may—or may not—help us understand it: a parable about yeast (leaven). (*Note:* If needed or desired, refer back to the comments in this Leader Guide, Session 2, regarding the possibility and value of thinking separately, as far as possible, about Jesus's parables and the settings in which the evangelists placed them.)

Read aloud both of these passages. You will want to tell participants that "three measures" is a large amount—between forty and sixty pounds. As Levine writes in chapter 3 of *Short Stories by Jesus*, "The dough would be far too much for one woman to knead on her own, and the yield would be far too much for one person to consume. The image is one of extravagance."

[Jesus] told them another parable: "The kingdom of heaven is like yeast that a woman took and mixed in with three measures of flour until all of it was leavened."

Matthew 13:33

And again [Jesus] said, "To what should I compare the kingdom of God? It is like yeast that a woman took and mixed in with three measures of flour until all of it was leavened."

Luke 13:20-21

Ask:

- How is the image of yeast like and unlike the image of the mustard seed?
- How is the extravagant result in this parable like and unlike the result at the end of the parable of the Mustard Seed?
- What does the parable of the Leaven suggest about the kingdom of God?
- Levine notes some interpretations of the parables of both the Mustard Seed and the Leaven encourage incorrect views of Judaism. For example, Jews did not and do not regard either mustard seeds or yeast as undesirable or "unclean"; therefore, these elements in Jesus's parables could not, for Jesus or his first-century Jewish audience, have represented "outsiders" or "undesirables" who were somehow threats to Judaism's system of ritual purity laws. Why do Christian readers need to remember that Jesus, a devout Jew, was not telling a parable that challenges the Jewish ritual purity system—which was, as Levine states, "one of the major concerns of Torah, of Jewish identity, and of the very practices that have kept Jews Jewish over the past two millennia"?
- Do you think the parable of the Leaven enhances our understanding of the parable of the Mustard Seed? Why or why not?

- How do you respond to Levine's interpretation of the two parables together: "Each shows that a single person's actions have a possible impact on life outside the immediate context; that is, the people who will come to eat the enormous amount of bread the woman has produced, and the birds that will nest in the branches of the tree"?

Tell participants that Mark places the parable of the mustard seed directly after another parable about a seed. Read aloud this passage:

> [Jesus] also said, "The kingdom of God is as if someone would scatter seed on the ground, and would sleep and rise night and day, and the seed would sprout and grow, he does not know how. The earth produces of itself, first the stalk, then the head, then the full grain in the head. But when the grain is ripe, at once he goes in with his sickle, because the harvest has come."
>
> Mark 4:26-29

Ask:

- How is the scattered seed in this parable like and unlike the mustard seed in the other parable?
- What other similarities and differences do you notice between the parables, and how are they significant?
- What does the parable of the Growing Seed suggest about the kingdom of God?
- Do you think the parable of the Growing Seed enhances our understanding of the parable of the Mustard Seed? Why or why not?

CALL TO ACTION

Read aloud these quotations from *Short Stories by Jesus*:

The parable does mark a contrast between small and great....It has something to say about seeds and birds, growth and shelter. These are the component parts of the parable, and it is from these that meanings may best be drawn.

No seed is, or should be, seen as insignificant; each contains life within it.

Even small actions, or hidden actions, have the potential to produce great things.

We are part of a larger process, and although we may start an action, once started, it can often do quite well on its own.

Ask:

- What assumptions does our society hold—and what assumptions do we as individuals hold—about who and what is "significant" and what actions matter that the Mustard Seed parable challenges?
- What might the parable suggest Christians, both as the church and as individuals, do in order to nurture the growth of the kingdom of God?
- What might the parable suggest Christians do *not* need to do in order to nurture the kingdom's growth?

Remind participants that the Lord's Prayer defines the coming of God's kingdom as God's will being done on earth as in heaven (Matthew 6:10). Encourage them to write down, on scrap paper, one action they either will *or will not* take this week in order to contribute to the growth of the kingdom.

OPTIONAL SESSION EXTENSION ACTIVITIES

If you think your group would enjoy extending the session with some activities they may remember from childhood, do one or both of the following to represent, as Levine writes, "humanity and nature work[ing] together" as the kingdom's growth:

Provide seeds, soil, and containers in which participants can plant a seed to take home with them and watch grow.

Depending upon the time of year, make feeders to help provide for "the birds of the air" by covering pine cones with peanut butter and birdseed and hanging them on tree branches with yarn.

CLOSING PRAYER

Close with this prayer or in your own words:

Loving God, giver of life and gracious provider, we praise you for calling us into your kingdom through your Son Jesus, and we pray that we will spread your loving rule through knowing when to act and when to wait upon you. Amen.

Session 5

The Laborers in the Vineyard

Session Goals

This session's reading, discussion, reflection, and prayer will equip participants to:

- explore the parable recorded in **Matthew 20:1-16**;
- appreciate the significance of vineyard imagery in Jewish Scripture;
- apply Jesus's parable to practical economic realities as well as to spiritual truths;
- commit themselves to practical acts of economic generosity.

Suggested Leader Preparation

Jesus my teacher, help me reflect your generosity in the ways I share my time, preparation, attention, enthusiasm, and love with the members of our study group, that we may grow together as your students and servants. Amen.

- Carefully and prayerfully read **Matthew 20:1-16** several times. Note words and phrases that attract your attention and meditate

on them. Write down questions about your reading and try to
find answers. If desired, consult a trusted Bible commentary.

- Carefully read *Short Stories by Jesus*, chapter 7. Note any material
  about which you need or want to do further research before the
  session.
- Carefully read Session 5 of the Participant Guide. Write down any
  questions or observations the material prompts.
- Secure and prepare a comfortable meeting space for your group,
  easily accessible to all participants regardless of physical ability.
- Materials needed: Bibles (especially in reputable translations not
  usually used by your group), scrap paper. *Optional:* name tags,
  hymnals, light refreshments, volunteer to read the parable aloud.
- Have a markerboard or pad of large paper on hand for writing
  down participants' responses, questions, and insights.
- Choose which discussion questions and activities you will use,
  keeping in mind your group's interests, previous Bible study
  experience, and comfort level with academic study (as opposed to
  purely devotional reading) of Scripture.

As Your Group Gathers

Welcome participants. Ask each to fill out and wear a name tag
(optional). Especially welcome any new participants. Invite participants
who have attended previous sessions to talk briefly about any new insights
they have gained or questions they are continuing to ponder.

Open with this prayer or pray in your own words:

*Energetic and industrious God, you are always creating and re-creating your
world and your people, and you call us to recognize and respond to your
work. May your Spirit guide our reading and reflecting today, that we may
learn more about working with you and welcoming your reign. We pray in the
name of our Savior, Jesus Christ. Amen.*

DESCRIBE "THE BEST BOSS" AND "THE WORST BOSS"

Ask participants to think about how they would complete this sentence: "The best boss I ever had…" After a few moments, invite volunteers to respond aloud. (Participants who have never been traditional employees could think and talk about the qualities they think someone worthy of the title "The Best Boss" would display, and why.) Write down key words, phrases, and ideas from participants' responses on the markerboard or large sheet of paper.

Repeat this exercise, thinking and talking about, "The worst boss I ever had…"

Encourage participants to bear this discussion in mind as they study the parable covered in this session.

HEAR AND REACT TO THE PARABLE

Recruit one volunteer to read aloud **Matthew 20:1-15**, while other group members listen without reading along in a Bible. (*Optional:* Contact someone prior to the session and ask her or him to prepare a public reading of the parable, encouraging this person to practice reading it with inflection and emotion. Choose someone who is a strong public speaker or a good storyteller, perhaps even someone with a background in theater, so that your group might hear the parable in a fresh, lively way.)

Ask:

- Imagine you were one of those hired to work at the beginning of the day. Would you have been "grumbling against the householder" who hired you when you received your wages? Why or why not?
- Imagine you were one of those hired to work just before the end of the day. How would you have reacted to receiving a denarius—a full day's wage—for such a short amount of work?
- Do you think the householder offers sufficient explanation and justification for the payments he gives? Why or why not?

- Based on how you heard this story, what do you think would be a good title for it?

STUDY THE PARABLE

Now have participants turn in their Bibles to **Matthew 20:1-15**. (As in previous sessions, you may wish to have on hand Bibles of a reputable translation your group does not usually use, or you may ask them to use Amy-Jill Levine's "fairly literal" translation in *Short Stories by Jesus*.) Recruit a different volunteer to read the parable aloud as the rest of the group follows along.

Ask:

- What words, phrases, or details did you notice in the second reading that you did not notice in the first? Why do you think they caught your attention this time?
- Levine notes that the word English Bibles often translate as "landowner" (verse 1, NRSV, CEB) is actually the Greek word for "householder" (*oikodespotes*), "master of a household." (Compare the same word in Matthew 24:43; Mark 14:14.) She argues that the "landowner" translation "increase[s] the possibility that [English-speaking Bible readers] will ... see the householder only as a figure for God." How might seeing the householder *first* as a literal human head of a household and "employer in search of labor" shape your understanding of the parable?
- Levine points out that, according to ancient Jewish sources, householders hiring laborers "cannot offer less than the going rate" for their location. In this case, a Roman denarius "would supply a family with three to six days of food." The householder agrees to pay this amount to the laborers because it is "right" ("just," "fair," "proper"). What does this agreement suggest about his ethical character?

- Levine also says translations of verses 3 and 6 suggesting that the laborers hired later were "idle" are not justified by the original Greek, which simply states they were "without work." And the text gives no reason for their lack of work except their statement, "no one has hired us" (verse 7). How do these details influence your understanding of the parable?
- What might the fact that the householder does not, at the day's beginning, accurately estimate how much labor he will need to gather the vineyard's harvest suggest about him?
- What might the fact that the workers hired first expect to be treated better than, not equally to, the workers hired last suggest about them?
- Levine writes, "The workers [who were hired earliest] seek what they perceive to be 'fair'; the householder teaches them a lesson by showing them what is 'right.'" When have you learned a lesson about the difference between what is fair and what is right? When have you taught or helped teach others such a lesson?
- The householder addresses one grumbling laborer as "friend." In another of Jesus's parables, this term is used for a guest who does not belong at a wedding banquet (Matthew 22:12), and Jesus calls his betrayer Judas "friend" in Gethsemane (26:50). How do these other uses of "friend" in Matthew influence the way we hear the householder using it?
- According to Levine, in ancient times "the evil eye" was regarded as a negative influence that possessed individuals. The householder's question to the grumbling laborers thus "gives them a possible out." What does the householder's response to the laborers suggest about him?
- Jesus's words in 20:16 about the last being first and vice versa are a "floating saying," attached to other parables and contexts in other Gospels (Mark 10:31; Luke 13:30) and even in

Matthew (19:30). Do you think it logically serves as a conclusion to this parable? Why or why not?

- Levine notes that interpreters are often resistant to reading this parable as a parable about ordinary economics, preferring instead to apply it to spiritual matters alone. What do you think may account for such resistance?
- Levine writes, "We can see in this householder a description of how ordinary householders do act or even should act." Do you agree? Why or why not?

EXAMINE THE IMAGE OF THE VINEYARD IN THE OLD TESTAMENT

Tell participants that although we need not understand the householder in the first place as a "stand-in" for God, "the possibility that the *oikodespotes* in [this] parable is a symbol for God should not be dismissed completely. Not all kings or vineyard owners in parables represent the divine, but some do." Tell participants that the vineyard would have been an image that might well have had religious resonance for this parable's original audience.

Form three groups. Assign each group one of the following Scriptures to read and discuss. Ask the groups to focus their discussions on what the vineyard in their assigned passage represents. (The parenthetical summaries in this list are provided for your benefit; you should share them with the groups only during the large group discussion afterward.)

- **Isaiah 5:1-7** (The prophet compares ancient Israel, which is being judged for injustice in its society, to a vineyard that does not produce the sweet fruit expected by the one who planted it.)
- **Psalm 80** (The psalm compares the people of Israel to a vine that God took from Egypt—a reference to the Exodus—and planted

in the Promised Land [verses 8-11]. The psalm also implores God to restore the vine [verses 3, 7]—the people have been damaged and defeated by enemies [verses 5-6, 12-13, 16a].)

- **Proverbs 24:30-34** (The overgrown "vineyard of a stupid person" becomes an object lesson in the importance of work.)

After allowing sufficient time for reading and discussion, invite a spokesperson from each group to summarize the group discussion. Ask each group these questions:

- What is the significance or the symbolism of the vineyard in your passage?
- What associations or connections, if any, do you imagine Jesus's original audience, assuming they knew the Scripture, might have made when they heard the mention of a vineyard in the parable about the laborers that he told?
- As Levine notes, some traditional interpretations of the parable of the laborers interpret the vineyard as a symbol for Israel, as it is in Isaiah 5 (among other Scriptures). These interpretations often conclude the story is (as Levine summarizes them) "a lesson of legalism versus grace," of "recalcitrant, always grumbling Jews, or at least their Pharisaic representatives, who sought to be judged by their 'works'" and who resent the acceptance of non-Jews into God's kingdom. Do you think the Old Testament passages we've looked at justify such interpretations? Why or why not?
- How much, if at all, do any of these Scriptures influence the way you interpret Jesus's parable of the laborers?

CALL TO ACTION

Read aloud these quotations from *Short Stories by Jesus*:

Maybe Jesus's parable *has* to do with economics after all.

Dismissing the parable's practical implication is to make the parable safe and so to lose its challenge.

If we refocus the parable away from "who gets into heaven" and toward "who gets a day's wage," we can find a message that challenges rather than prompts complacency. If we look at economics, at the pressing reality that people need jobs and that others have excess funds, we find what should be a compelling challenge to any hearer. And in that story, we learn what it means to act as God acts, with generosity to all.

Ask:

- If we read this parable as a lesson in "what it means to act as God acts," what might we infer from it about Jesus's definition of "the best boss"?
- When have you seen people with economic advantage acting with deliberate, life-sustaining generosity, as the householder in the parable does?

Encourage participants to write down on scrap paper one practical way in which they will show economic generosity in the coming week.

Closing Prayer

Close with this prayer or in your own words:

Ever-living, ever-giving God: may your Spirit move us to act with generosity, being especially generous toward those who have little in a world where others have too much. Make us restless for a world where, as in your kingdom to come, all have what they need to live. Stir us to make changes, beginning in our own lives, for the sake and glory of your Son, Jesus Christ. Amen.

Session 6

The Widow and the Judge

SESSION GOALS

This session's reading, discussion, reflection, and prayer will equip participants to:

- explore both the parable recorded in **Luke 18:1-8** and Luke's framing interpretation of it;
- consider how stereotypes prevent us from viewing and treating others as real people;
- commit to taking a practical step toward reconciliation, in their personal lives or in society;
- reflect on how their study of *Short Stories by Jesus* has influenced the way they read and interpret Jesus's parables.

SUGGESTED LEADER PREPARATION

Jesus my teacher, thank you for the opportunity to serve your people as a group leader. Bless our last gathering as this group with a fresh appreciation of Scripture, a new encounter with your Word, and a renewed commitment to live as Jesus's followers, seeking your just and righteous kingdom above all. Amen.

- Carefully and prayerfully read **Luke 18:1-8** several times. Note words and phrases that attract your attention and meditate on them. Write down questions about your reading and try to find answers. If desired, consult a trusted Bible commentary.
- Carefully read *Short Stories by Jesus*, chapter 8 and the conclusion, "The Power of Disturbing Stories." Note any material about which you need or want to do further research before the session.
- Carefully read Session 6 of the Participant Guide. Write down any questions or observations the material prompts.
- Secure and prepare a comfortable meeting space for your group, easily accessible to all participants regardless of physical ability.
- Materials needed: Bibles (especially in reputable translations not usually used by your group), scrap paper. *Optional:* name tags, hymnals, light refreshments, volunteer to read the parable aloud.
- Have a markerboard or pad of large paper on hand for writing down participants' responses, questions, and insights.
- Choose which discussion questions and activities you will use, keeping in mind your group's interests, previous Bible study experience, and comfort level with academic study (as opposed to purely devotional reading) of Scripture.

As Your Group Gathers

Welcome participants. Ask each to fill out and wear a name tag (optional). Especially welcome any participants who have not attended previous sessions.

Open with this prayer or pray in your own words:

Almighty God, high and lifted up: you seek justice in this unjust world, and you demand your people pursue it. As we read and reflect on Jesus's parable today, send your Spirit to help us hear the Scriptures with new ears, and to kindle again our desire to live with the righteousness that you command. Amen.

IDENTIFY SYMBOLS OF JUSTICE

Lead participants in brainstorming a list of familiar symbols or images of justice (for example: a courthouse; Lady Justice blindfolded and holding scales; a judge with a robe and a gavel). Encourage participants with smartphones or other mobile devices to find pictures of these symbols.

Ask:

- Which of these symbols most strongly represents justice for you? Why?
- How do you define justice?
- What is the difference between justice and vengeance?
- How closely do you think God's definition of justice matches human definitions of justice, and why?

Encourage participants to keep these images and reflections in mind as they read and discuss this session's parable.

HEAR AND REACT TO THE PARABLE

Recruit a volunteer to read aloud **Luke 18:2-5**, while the rest of the group listens without reading along in their Bibles.

After the reading, ask:

- Who are the characters in this parable?

- Do you respond to one of these characters more favorably than the other? If so, which one and why? If not, why not?
- Based on what you have heard, what would you title this parable?

STUDY THE PARABLE

Now have participants turn in their Bibles to **Luke 18**. (As in previous sessions, you may wish to have on hand Bibles of a reputable translation your group does not usually use, or you may ask them to use Amy-Jill Levine's "fairly literal" translation in *Short Stories by Jesus*.) Instruct the group to read **verses 2-5 only**.

Ask:

- What does the parable itself tell us directly about the judge and the widow?
- Read **Proverbs 1:7** and **Leviticus 19:14**. What do you think the judge's lack of "the fear of the Lord" reveals about him?
- Read **Luke 20:13-14**. What do you think the judge's "not respecting" people reveals about him?
- As Levine notes, the Greek text—contrary to most English translations—says the widow is not seeking "justice" but is seeking to be "avenged." This legal term "could be positive or at least morally neutral," but it carries overtones of punishment and judgment in the New Testament (for example: Romans 12:19; 2 Corinthians 10:6; Revelation 19:2) and the Greek translation of the Old Testament (for example: Genesis 4:15; Exodus 7:4; Numbers 31:2; Deuteronomy 32:43). How does the widow's request for vengeance influence your opinion of her?
- How does the fact that the parable includes no details about why the widow wants to be avenged affect your understanding of it?
- Does the lack of detail about the widow's opponent influence your understanding?

- Translating literally from the Greek, according to Levine, the judge says the widow keeps "causing me labor" and worries she will eventually "beat me up"—the term comes from boxing (compare 1 Corinthians 9:27). How do the judge's motivations influence your reactions to him—and to the widow?
- Which of your previous assumptions, if any, about the parable's characters are not directly supported by verses 2-5? How and why do you think you developed these assumptions?
- Based on these verses alone, what would you say this parable is really about? What meaning(s) would you take away from it?

STUDY LUKE'S CONTEXT FOR THE PARABLE

Remind participants that this study of *Short Stories by Jesus* seeks to examine Jesus's parables in what is as close as we can come to their original forms before considering them in the contexts provided by the evangelists. (You may wish to refer to comments on this subject in Session 2.)

Invite participants to read **Luke 18:1-8.**

Ask:

- Why do you think Luke introduces this parable as he does in verse 1?
- In verse 6, how does Jesus characterize the judge? Do you think the parable itself suggests the judge is necessarily "unjust"? Why or why not?
- How does Jesus say God is like or unlike the judge in the parable (verses 6-8)?
- How do you relate Jesus's comment about the Son of Man in verse 8 to the parable?
- Levine concludes that Luke's frame around this parable "doesn't work" and "doesn't help." Do you agree? Why or why not?

- How is this parable in its current setting like and unlike the parable Jesus tells and the lesson he teaches in **Luke 11:5-8**?
- How likely do you think it is that Jesus originally told this parable to teach the lesson he teaches in verses 7-8? Why?
- Do you find the parable of the judge and the widow encourages you in your own praying? Why or why not?

STUDY SCRIPTURE ABOUT WIDOWS

Form six small groups of participants. Assign each group one of the following Scriptures to read. Instruct each group to discuss this question, which you may want to write on the markerboard or large sheet of paper: "What view of widows does this text present?" (The parenthetical summaries in this list are provided for your benefit; you should only share them with the groups during the large group discussion afterward.)

- **Psalm 146:5-9** (God's faithfulness is seen in God giving justice to people who are vulnerable, including widows.)
- **Deuteronomy 24:19-21** and **27:19** (God commands God's people to provide economic support for those who need it, including widows.)
- **Isaiah 1:16-17** (Through the prophet, God calls God's people to "do good," which includes "plead[ing] for the widow," assuming that widows could or did not plead for themselves.)
- **James 1:27** (The apostle defines pure religion as including "car[ing] for orphans and widows in their distress.")
- **Luke 2:36-38** (The prophet Anna is persistent in prayer and proclaims to others what God is doing through the child Jesus.)
- **Luke 21:1-4** (Jesus notes that a poor widow chooses to offer all she has to God at the Temple.)

Have a representative from each group talk about highlights of the small group discussions. Ask the whole group:

- What do these Scriptures about widows have in common? How do they differ?
- How is the widow in the parable of the Widow and the Judge like and unlike the widows in these Scriptures?
- How much or how little should other Scriptures about widows influence the way we understand Jesus's parable? Why?
- "Telling a widow in a church today that she is helpless, oppressed, or needy may not be good news," notes Levine. "It may also not be accurate." How do these Scriptures contribute to or challenge stereotypical attitudes about widows?
- Levine writes, "The Jewish widows we know from [ancient] legal documents were necessarily neither helpless nor cast into the street. The same point holds for widows who were among the followers of Jesus.... Some widows no doubt were destitute, but to conclude that widow abuse was the dominant pattern is to overstate the case." How could assuming more than the parable actually tells us about the widow's social and economic status contribute, even inadvertently, to anti-Jewish beliefs and attitudes?
- Levine also writes, "At the very least, [this parable] calls into question stereotypes of widows and judges.... Once our stereotypes are shattered, we can begin to look at people as individuals rather than as social roles." How does the widow in Jesus's story shatter stereotypes about widows we may hold, even those rooted in Scripture?
- How much, if at all, does viewing the widow in the parable as an individual, rather than as an example of stereotypical "widows," change your understanding of the story?

CALL TO ACTION

Read aloud this quotation from *Short Stories by Jesus*:

The parable disturbs... because the only form of closure it creates is that in which widow and judge—and so readers—become complicit in a plan possibly to take vengeance and certainly not to find reconciliation. We may resist that complicity and so opt out of the system that promotes it. We may decide that court cases are not worth our time, that compassion is less time consuming and less corrupting than vengeance. Our task may be to resist the parable rather than rescue it.

Ask:

- How do you react to the idea that our task may be resisting this parable?
- What might these Scriptures have to tell us about resisting a system that does not produce justice: **Matthew 5:43-48; Luke 12:57-59; 1 Corinthians 6:1-8**?
- What are some situations in society today where justice and reconciliation are needed?
- What is the difference between justice and vengeance? Can you think of any situations in which the distinction is not entirely clear?
- How does your church (your congregation and/or your denomination) work for justice and reconciliation in society?
- How do you work for justice and reconciliation in your own life?

Invite participants to write on scrap paper one practical action they will take this week that contributes to justice and reconciliation, whether in their personal lives or in society.

REFLECT ON THE STUDY

Remind participants that this is the final session of your group's study of *Short Stories by Jesus*. Thank them for their participation.

Ask:

- What is the most interesting, memorable, or provocative thing you have learned during our study?
- How much, if at all, has this study changed the way you read Jesus's parables?
- Which other parables of Jesus are you most interested in reading and studying, having completed this study?

Closing Prayer

Close with this prayer or in your own words:

Holy God, we thank you for continuing to challenge us through the parables of your Son, Jesus, who became for us wisdom from on high. Even as we proclaim him as Savior, may we never forget how his disciples also called him "Teacher," and may your Spirit keep us always open to his lessons about what it means to truly live—not only in the world to come, but in this world that you have given all people—as those who know and do your will. Amen.

9 781501 858185

CPSIA information can be obtained
at www.ICGtesting.com
Printed in the USA
LVHW032339220822
726336LV00002B/4

9 781501 858185